When there are no Words:

25 Prayers for the Transition from Life to Eternity

Prayers

1. Prayer for the Dying
2. Prayer for Grieving
3. Prayer to Release Anger
4. Prayer for Joy
5. Prayer for Light
6. Prayer for Stress
7. Prayer for Good Report
8. Prayer for Bad Report
9. Prayer for Understanding
10. Prayer for the Unknown Adventure
11. Prayer for the Known Adventure
12. Prayer for before the diagnoses
13. Prayer for after the diagnoses
14. Prayer for when there is Nothing that Can be Done
15. Prayer for Treatment Days
16. Prayer for Family Peace in Troubled Times
17. Prayer for Happy Days
18. Prayer of Gratefulness
19. Prayer for Grieving what was
20. Prayer for Caregivers
21. Prayer for Medical Team
22. Prayer to make the right decisions
23. Prayer of Daily Protection
24. Prayer for Peace
25. Prayer for this New Life

Dedication

For my dad Rudy

1957-2019

My Grandmother Mozelle Cortes

1930-2022

My Grandfather Alberto Cortes

1933-2021

Thank you for teaching me the power of prayer and faith in our Lord and Savior.

Till we meet again,

I love you.

About the Author:

Alyssa S. Cortes-Kennedy is a native South Texan. She is a 1st generation college graduate with a B.A. in criminal justice from the University of Texas at San Antonio and a master's in administration from the University of the Incarnate Word. She is currently a doctoral candidate for a Ph.D. in education, with a concentration in organizational leadership and a specialty in adult learning and teaching at UIW. Her administration and leadership passions stem from a military family history and working in large and small business, which include legal, medical, and corporate America areas. She is an ambitious and active advocate for life-long learning, cancer awareness and research (specifically, Glioblastoma), veterans' education (at all stages of service), and the application of faith and duty as a global citizen. If asked, Alyssa would say first, she is a follower of Jesus Christ, a wife, daughter, sister, granddaughter, dog mom, and world traveler.

Introduction:

The journey of losing a loved one, for some, is often felt at the beginning of a serious diagnoses and is drawn out well before your loved one passes away. For others, not given time, grief is felt differently when death is unexpected. However, when death is inevitably coming emotions are on a never ending roller-coaster of ups and downs, twists, and turns, and yes, maybe some nauseousness throughout the ride, literally and figuratively. Each journey is different and with those differences but there are similar emotions each of us go through and carry well after our loved one has passed. The journey through a terminal illness is one few, yet many can empathize with. Prayer for most is a comfort, even for those who have never prayed a day in their life, suddenly feel the need to pray or feel a positive force over their life in moments of uncertainty. Prayer for this author was and is a necessity to understanding and accepting the circumstances of the experience.

In my personal experiences with loved ones passing, I have often become anger, sad, discouraged and helplessly worn out. The transition from this physical world to the eternal afterlife is often questioned. Caregivers and loved ones often ask themselves "Am I making the right decision?", "What would I have done differently?", "Is this what my husband wanted?", "Why do I feel alone in this fight?", "Why doesn't anyone understand that I am still grieving?". These are just a few of the questions I and my own family have had in our experience of loss and grief. This prayer book reflects my own prayers to which I often wrote down throughout my dad's brain cancer battle and passing, my mother's throat cancer, and my maternal grandparents passing within one year of each other during a global pandemic. This prayer book's purpose is to help those going through similar situations pray when they cannot find the words. Giving them something to stand on when there is nothing left to do or give. My hope is, it gives you a voice when you just don't know what to do.

    I have been told or asked, "you're so strong!", "how do you get through so much?", "how can you have faith with so much loss?", "How do you do it?". To which I reply. Faith! Jesus! The Lamb. Tears. Prayers. Sometimes back to a lot of tears! Sometimes a lot of Prayers. Sometimes, I do not know! But I do know I am here by the one above. What I have learned is that acceptance is peace. Because within acceptance and peace comes understanding that this is not the end. It is the end in a physical form but the beginning of forever in the spiritual realm. This book of prayers is not meant to make you accept you or your loved one's circumstances and move on like nothing is or has happened, but to give you the words when you just don't have anymore. When all the prayers have been said, or perhaps you're turning to prayer for the first time. It is meant to remind you, you are not alone, there is power in prayer. There is power in the words you speak. While we cannot control what will ultimately happen, we can control how we look at our forever. May these prayers uplift you and be a refuge for you.

I will praise Him in the Good, I will Praise Him in the Bad, in ALL these praised be the name of the Lord.

To God be the Glory.

-A

1. Prayer for the Dying

My God, My Savior, My Eternity,

I am dying maybe today, or tomorrow, maybe not for a while, but I know you are soon calling me home.

Lord, protect my soul, guide me to your eternal light. Let me hear the angels sing and guide me along my journey.

I am not afraid Lord, for I know you are with me. I know your promise to be true and I know where I am going.

I have been saved by your grace and through that my soul will continue past the boundaries in this physical world.

Lord, give my family peace and understanding that I am and will be ok. If I do worry, it is for them. If it be your will allow me to check in on them when I am gone. Let me be to send them signs of love and to let them know I am ok.

When the time come Lord, I will be ready and I know I will be ok, until then give me a song to sing in my heart and a testimony to tell of your enduring love.

You are my refuge.

Amen.

Date(s) prayed:

Why did I prayer this today?

2. Prayer for Grieving

Dear Lord,

This grief is too much.

Somedays are good and many are bad right now.

I am on an emotional roller coaster.

Please let the people around me have patience, let me have patience.

Grant me your grace Lord to look to the future. To know that my loved one is resting in your enteral love.

This is hard Lord. I don't know how to handle to emotions I have. I mourn for them, for me, for everyone who is missing them.

Lord, cover me in a blanket of love. I feel alone, sad, confused.

Help me in this life without the one I love next to me.

Help me to find my place again and to continue on my journey.

Amen.

Date(s) prayed:

Why did I prayer this today?

3. Prayer to Release Anger

Father,

Let me feel your presence in this moment.

A moment when I feel so anger at my surroundings.

When nothing seems to be going well.

Let me be slow to raise my voice, think before I react.

Give me peace when at this moment I feel none.

Give me signs to know I am making the right decisions.

To be calm under pressure, and not react.

Lord, help me to release what is needed and to see your grace in all that is happening.

Amen.

Date(s) prayed:

Why did I prayer this today?

4. Prayer for Joy

Lord,

Thank you for the gift of joy.

Thank you for letting me wake up this morning and feel your presence.

Thank you for giving me the spirit of joy.

To feel the light and life I have within me.

I thank you for letting me feel like me today.

To see the blue sky, hear cheer and laugher, and be at peace.

Let this joy radiate to all of those who I encounter today.

May they feel your spirit within me.

Date(s) prayed:

Why did I prayer this today?

5. Prayer for Light

Heavenly Father,

Let my life be an extension of your love father God.

Be with me all my days, through the good and the bad.

When I am feeling sick hold me in the palm of your hand.

Heal me O' Lord from the top of my head to the soles of my feet, from the inside, out.

Let me see the finish line, the light at the end of this tunnel. Be my steadfast.

This is my prayer.

Friday, August 13, 2021

Date(s) prayed:

Why did I prayer this today?

6. Prayer for Stress

Precious Lord,

My heart is racing.

My mind is working overtime.

I am worried Lord.

I know this worry is not from you, but of this world.

Help me to see your ways in this stressful time.

Help me to seek your wisdom and not the wisdom of an unpredictable world.

When I am up thinking and stressing of the things to come, comfort me, guide me.

Be with me when I cannot seem to calm down and see the light.

Help me to slow down, breath and be one with your spirit.

Remind me you are in control and there is no need to fear.

Praise be your name.

Date(s) prayed:

Why did I prayer this today?

7. Prayer for Good Report

Dearest Heavenly Father,

Thank you for a good report.

Thank you that these treatments are working.

Thank you for giving me a team and family who supports my every need.

Thank you, that you are guiding the teams to treat me properly.

You are in the midst of these good days, and I will praise you every step of the way.

Thank you that you already see the good and it topples the bad.

You are the God of second chances, the one who makes us whole.

I will praise you all my days.

Date(s) prayed:

Why did I prayer this today?

8. Prayer after a Bad Report

Heavenly Father,

I am at a loss.

I don't know what to say, ask for, or do.

All I can do is come to you heart and soul wide open.

I can't lie, Lord I'm having a hard time. I do not understand. Nor may I ever.

I feel lost, I feel let down, I feel I have nothing else to hope for.

Give me peace.

Give me love and let me give love.

Give me hope, gracious healer.

While my healing may not be in the form I thought, I am still trusting in you for it.

Heal me in the form you fill is fit for me.

Let me find the good in the bad.

Let me be still and be with you amid my sadness.

You are still in control, and I will trust you every step of the way.

Date(s) prayed:

Why did I prayer this today?

9. Prayer for Understanding

Lord,

I come to you asking for clarity.

I need to understand what is happening.

And while I may not have or get all the answers, I want to feel present to be the I can be.

To do the best I can do.

Give my family understanding and bless them Lord for standing alongside me.

Give my friends understanding when I can no longer be there to comfort their needs.

Give my physicians or caregivers understanding to guide me properly, but to give me grace when I am frustrated or confused.

Be with us Lord, the center of our discussions and our praise, all our days.

Date(s) prayed:

Why did I prayer this today?

10. Prayer for the Unknown Adventure

Gracious Creator,

When I think of my life journey there is NO way I would be where I am without salvation through your son Jesus Christ.

It is him who is my rock.

My Fortress.

My deliverance is through his promises.

He is my light; he is my promise.

Without Him I would be a lost soul.

I do not know what the future hold; But I know who holds the future and it is well with my soul.

I will go where you want me to go, I will be where you want me to be.

I will trust in the Lord forever and always.

My soul is yours God. You are my God, and I am your child.

I will trust you through this unknown journey.

Amen.

Monday, July 27, 2020
2:45 PM

Date(s) prayed:

Why did I prayer this today?

11. Prayer for the Known Adventure

Lord,

I know where I am headed.

I have made my plans and them have been confirmed.

I praise you for being with me on this journey.

I pray for wisdom to know the path I am on and where I am going.

For you have created them long before me.

Lord, give me peace on this adventure.

For some adventures are known as this one is and you will be in the midst of it.

I praise you for favor.

I praise you for protection.

I thank you for this adventure.

In your name I pray these things.

Date(s) prayed:

Why did I prayer this today?

12. Prayer for before the diagnoses

Dear God, my Creator,

I do not know the results of my tests or my diagnoses.

I think I have an idea, but you know the truth.

I pray you give wisdom to my doctors and technicians to diagnose me correctly.

I pray you give them patience when they explain things to me.

I pray that I know how to respond and stay collected.

I pray that my family understands when it is time to explain things to them.

Lord, help me to know that no matter what you are in control and only you hold the ultimate answers to my journey.

Where I am headed is in your hands.

I will trust you.

I will lean only on your words and promises.

For I am made whole and in the image of my creator.

For unto you I will live my days to their fullest.

Amen.

Date(s) prayed:

Why did I prayer this today?

13. Prayer for after the diagnoses

Dearest Lord,

Here I am with these diagnoses.

Be with me, as I know you are.

Help me on this journey Lord.

Give me patience, understanding, and faith.

I pray for my family, that they will understand.

I pray that I will continue to understand my doctors.

That they will be near when I need their understanding.

That they will be patient.

Lord, give me the strength to endure what I can.

When I cannot be my strength.

Be my joy when I have none.

Be my hope when it is faint.

I trust you.

Praise. Be your name.

Date(s) prayed:

Why did I prayer this today?

14. Prayer for when there is Nothing that Can be Done

Dearest Lord,

This_____ is a disease.

A disease that has come to with a vengeance.

A disease which seeks to kill all it touches.

Its ipact is deeper than the cells in my (or loved one's body).

Its roots are heavy and twisted, they hurt the good cells and good people.

I do not understand why.

My family is hurting, other patients are hurting, others seem to know my own hurt and disappointment but ignore my pain.

I know life will go on. Give me peace.

My people will go on. Give them peace.

Lord, help me to stay still, listen, breathe, as if I am stuck in time. Help me to see the things around me even though I feel stuck. As things go on, help me Lord as I stay still.

I believe in your will.

Amen.

Sunday, August 29, 2021
9:20 PM

Date(s) prayed:

Why did I prayer this today?

15. Prayer for Treatment Days

God,

Today I have treatment.

Touch my mind and spirit to remain strong through this trial.

Bless my medical team to administer the medication correctly.

Bless their souls to be kind and remember I am alone human.

I have emotions and may have some fear.

I believe you will be in control.

And while I do not understand why I am going through this.

All I will and can do is pray for my healing and believe in your power

as the great physician.

I love you, Lord.

I bless your Holy name 100x100.

-Amen

Saturday, August 7, 2021

Date(s) prayed:

Why did I prayer this today?

16. Prayer for Family Peace in Troubled Times

Dear God,

My family is at odds.

I pray for peace amongst us.

I pray for patience between one another.

We are all struggling with our emotions.

We are fearful, even though we shouldn't be.

It's hard Lord, I don't have answers for them, but I know you do!

I will trust in your will, and I pray they are accepting of that.

I know you are the almighty and everything will be ok.

Remind us of your loved for your son Jesus and let us love one another like you do your son.

Let us be reminded we are on the same team. I cast division to the sea and call on unity for my family.

This is hard God! I cannot, we cannot do this on our own so I lean on you for peace in my family during this troubled time.

Amen.

Date(s) prayed:

Why did I prayer this today?

17. Prayer for Happy Days

Dear Lord,

Today is a good day.

Thank you.

I hear the birds; I see the sun shining and the breeze flowing through the trees.

I am alive because of you.

I am healthy minded.

I am praising you for all you have done.

In your bigger plan you still had time to create me.

Today I am happy.

Let me continue to have this joyfulness in my heart all of my days.

For unto you I sing my praises.

Amen.

Date(s) prayed:

Why did I prayer this today?

18. Prayer of Gratefulness

Lord,

I am so grateful today.

Thank you for waking me up again today.

Thank you for your mercy, strength, and love.

Thank you, no matter, what the day brings.

I am grateful for another chance in this world.

My circumstances are different, but I am grateful for your guidance through it all.

I am grateful for favor.

I am grateful for love.

I am grateful for hope.

I am grate for the cross.

Amen.

Date(s) prayed:

Why did I prayer this today?

19. Prayer for Grieving what was

Heavenly Father,

I do not recognize this life I am living right now.
Everything seems to have gone away.
I feel lost, I feel weak, I feel alone.
I do not recognize myself, or others around me.
I feel the life I had before slipped away in the blink of an eye.
Why Lord?
I do not understand.
While I know I may never, help me to accept what is my journey.
Help me to begin to live again, a new normal.
Help me to recognize whatever that may be.
Remind me of all the good memories I have in my past seasons of life.
That they may bring me joy and not pain.
Lord, I am grieving what was...it hurts. I miss my "normal".
Be with me in this new season.
Be with me as I begin again.

Amen.

Date(s) prayed:

Why did I prayer this today?

20. Prayer for Caregivers

Dear God,

As I set into my role as caregiver give me the tools I need to get through the day.

Give me patience when tempers flare.

Give me physical strength to help uphold my loved one.

Give me knowledge to make the right decision for they want, and not my needs.

Hold me accountable to be their strength when needed.

Let others see me and hear me and not downplay my role.

Lord, give us a good day. A day where we make memories, even in the middle of a busy schedule.

Give me rest Lord, because sometimes it is too much.

Be with me, protect me, guide me in your will.

Amen.

Date(s) prayed:

Why did I prayer this today?

21. Prayer for Medical Team

Greatest Physician,

Surround me with knowledgeable medical professionals.

Lord, as they look at the tests, give them strategy for good.

Allow my doctors to recall all their knowledge in this moment.

Guide their hands during the procedures Lord.

Let them be led only by you.

Let me be a light to my medical team Lord.

Even in my sickness, use me as a testimony of your grace.

Bless them with rest, calm spirits and understanding.

Let them see me first, as a human being and then as a patient.

Let them have the answers to the best of your protective hand.

Be with them Lord as they intervene to physically help me.

In your Holy Name.

Date(s) prayed:

Why did I prayer this today?

22. Prayer to make the right decisions

Dear Lord,

Be with me as I make these decisions.

There are many Lord and I don't know exactly what to do.

I ask you:

Give me clarity to make the right decisions for me/my loved one.

Give me peace before, during, and after I make these decisions.

Calm my Spirit, let me feel your presence.

Lord, Have your divine way.

Heal me, Lord.

Finally, deliver me from what or whom may be against me in this battle of choices.

I trust you, Lord.

Tuesday, August 17, 2021

Date(s) prayed:

Why did I prayer this today?

23. Prayer of Daily Protection

Gracious Lord,

Be with me in the valley and on the mountain top.

It is dark, sometimes there is light. Guide my way, make a path.

Charge the army of God, the saints, and my guardian angels to walk

before me, beside me, behind me, and all the way through.

I trust you, Lord.

I give you all glory, honor, and praise

for all my days.

Amen.

Wednesday, August 18, 2021

Date(s) prayed:

Why did I prayer this today?

24. Prayer for Peace

Father,

Create in me a peaceful journey.

Create in me a peaceful heart.

Create in me a hope for a new tomorrow.

Keep me calm and give me comfort.

Let me be at ease with whatever may be.

Give me a light to pass to others when they look to me to create peace.

Lord, I do not have everything but through you I know nothing is impossible.

Thank you, Father.

Peace, you give and peace I will receive.

Amen.

Date(s) prayed:

Why did I prayer this today?

25. Prayer for this New Life

Dearest Creator,

You have given us a new journey.

This unexpected loop in our path.

For this new life I praise you.

While I adjust and try to understand be my guide.

Help me to overcome doubt.

Help me to be accepting.

Help me to be bold.

Thank you for what you have done.

Thank you for a new start.

Thank you for helping me along the way.

I do not understand, but I will still sing your praises.

For you are my Lord thy God.

For whom I will stand for all my days.

With Love and a grateful heart, I pray these things.

Date(s) prayed:

Why did I prayer this today?

www.ingramcontent.com/pod-product-compliance
Lightning Source LLC
LaVergne TN
LVHW051203080426
835508LV00021B/2783